Tom Denbigh lives in Bristol with an obscene number of books. He is the first Bristol Pride Poet Laureate and a BBC 1Extra Emerging Artist Talent Search winner. He has performed at the Royal Albert Hall and festivals around the UK, and has brought poetry to Brighton and London Prides. He is a producer at Milk Poetry and has facilitated writing workshops for groups of students from the UK and abroad (he is particularly proud of his work with young queer people). Outside of poetry Tom is a doctor with a PhD in plant roots and crumbling soil. He now works on climate change policy.

...and then she ate him

Tom Denbigh

Burning Eye

BurningEyeBooks
Never Knowingly Mainstream

LOTTERY FUNDED

Supported using public funding by
ARTS COUNCIL ENGLAND

This edition published by Burning Eye Books 2018

www.burningeye.co.uk

@burningeyebooks

Burning Eye Books
15 West Hill, Portishead, BS20 6LG

ISBN 978-1-911570-72-1

For Joy

Contents

FAGGOT

INNOCENT

VILLAIN

INTRODUCTION

I don't tend to read poetry books in order. Often when I read poems I read a few at once; I pick a collection up, pull some out and hold them with me for the next few days.

I wanted to write a book which would work for me, but also for those people (who I will never understand) who like to go directly from A to B.

This book is divided up into sections, which are named after the characters that you meet in stories. Traditionally, there are six character archetypes. I've stuck with this and now present to you a mix of traditional and novel characters to keep you company. It's up to you whether you meet them one after the other or, for example, decide to go straight to the Trickster, because really it's mischief you are in the mood for today.

However you read poetry books, I hope you enjoy this one.

WITCH

SIREN

for Siân

'What are you reading?' he asks,
hovering by her table,
despite the title of her book,
I Wish You'd Fuck Off and Leave Me Alone –
sorry,
Gone Girl –
being very visible on the front.

'Gone Girl,'
she says,
pointing at the cover
and smiling far more politely than she needs to.

'I love a girl who reads,' he says.
She smiles again,
staccato,
eyes fixed on horizon,
then back to page.

'Do you read a lot?'
he asks.

'Yes,'
she says,
a mistake
which is mistaken
for an invitation.

He sits.

'The last **book** I read,'
he says
(emphasising the word **book**
so she knows he means *book-book*
and not just... book),

'The last **book** I read
was *Mice and Men*
for A-level,
but I just haven't had time
with my *start-up*, you see.'

He dangles his *start-up*
like bait,
swinging it
in front of her face.
From the flashed
wrinkle of her nose
it is no more appealing.

'You know, you look like someone who reads,'
he says,
sliding along her booth,
which is marooned
at the back
of the café
out of sight of the waitress.

'Yeah,'
he says,
eyes lingering on her cardigan
and glasses,
lip curling like a wave,
'you look like someone who… reads.'

She blinks,
one of those long ones
that causes gulls to fly into windows in panic
and rats to leave a ship.

The smell of seaweed floats in the air.

It looks like her book
is the decaying carcass of a seabird
strung about her neck,

but really
that suits her
just
fine.

'I was wondering, actually,'
she says
quietly,
'if you could help me with *this* word.'
He grins,
finally,
slips his serpent arm
about her
and peers at the page.

It reads
submerged.

He stares.
It is not a hard word
and for a second he wonders
if she is joking with him,
but this thought is interrupted
with the prick of teeth on his elbow
as she unhinges her jaw,
circumnavigates his torso with her pin-sharp fangs
and with a single cavernous gulp
takes his whole body inside her
just like he wanted.

*

Five minutes later
the waitress
steers round the corner
to see how the reader is doing.
As she asks for 'another cup of tea, please,'
the door rings open
and a man walks in

with a certain gait.
She coughs politely,
wipes her mouth,
adjusts her hair
so she looks exactly like a *girl who reads*
and pushes out an aura
of
do not disturb.

She pauses.
It is almost too easy.
Silence these days
is far more tempting
than any song.

ITCH

maybe
every time the magic comes back
springing forth in that second after
the last beat of a lamb's heart
or the moment before the mother ewe's cry
always with blood and desperation
and hard-earned
twice-paid

maybe
every time it comes back
after that

suddenly

pixies replace flies
thrumming against windows
jabbering with shrill blue tongues
as twelve-year-olds stand open-mouthed
and broomsticks twitch with mischief

maybe then
we have to learn the rules again
to not walk widdershins around a grave
or forget the saucer of milk in the kitchen for the phooka
or leave windows open over cradles
obviously

though
when the world is oozing with magic
swollen and gravid
it's easy to wish it gone once more
entropic

and
not from fear of thorned prisons and dragons
but out of irritation

with the sour milk and broken china
scudding across kitchen floors
or at the sight of dry blue bodies
twisted on windowsills
we close our eyes
and wish for flies again

GREEN

To a witch, from his love.

The first time,
staring across the rooftops,
I saw you
crouched in a tiled valley
as you sang pigeons' feet
from broken vees back to scaled forks.
I must have cooed too
because you jerked your eyes to peer,
stumbled for a second
and slipped,
pulling clods of green from the roof.
For a second you were more moss than man,
swampthing
and hilarious
and then
in a breath
gone.
When I came back to the same spot a week later
the moss was back,
more emerald than ever,
and sewn in place
with small white flowers.

The second time
I think you saw me first
by the old canal at that thinness of town and country.
I was fishing folded bottles from the murk
until I saw your flick of grin below the rotten water
and then it was my turn to slip,
though as I fell I think I saw your feet,
silver with bubbles or scales;
I'm still not sure which.
The freshwater laughter of your flirtation
echoed.

Months later,
in my allotment,
I had ceased looking,
was kneeling, sowing seed –
your arm snaked round mine,
hand closing over my whole body.
With reverence,
we sowed together.

You showed me how the oldest trees still remember the tales
their grandmothers told of the endless forest
that stretched where concrete crouches now,
like cliffs driven inshore.

You showed me which berries grew too close to car exhausts,
gave me a mushroom from the old church gutter,
the softest thing I have ever held,
and brought me to where you lived
between burnt-out buildings –
a clasp of green
that you could only reach by climbing.

I was a slow learner
as you showed me how to make old wood wake,
to sing blackbird feathers into breezes,
taught me to slip behind the eyes of strangers,
like the foxes taught you once, you said,
long ago.

I remember how one afternoon
the sky swollen with storm
had split.
We waited
in the nest of the solitary bee
and then, as clouds parted,
ran to the highest building,
wove fresh sunlight round our fingers
and then fled
down and deep and long

till we reached the buried rivers beneath,
sleeping and hungry,
and stirred sunbeams
into their winding bodies,
warming them.
I remember how they shuddered,
gasped at the overdue feeding,
began to wake,
how we whispered in that hissing water-speak,
'Not now, but not long yet,'
and cried in empty caves.

To a love, from his witch.

I had forgotten more than I realised,
much like those rivers,
had nearly become nothing more than moss myself,
a breeze,
the shape of dust left by wings,
till the golden of your laughter stirred life into me.

That day when I held you
you told me your name,
which I saw no need for;
I knew your smell,
the sound your thoughts made,
the colour of your smile.
But later, when it beaded on my lips, in boiling orgasm,
I realised your name was declaration
and song
all at once.

I was slow to trust; I regret that now
but watched as you watched me.
Taught you to mend the wings
of earwigs
with silk
and moonlight.
You taught me too

how to peel the slabs of spikes
from tree branches,
to melt that glue that stank of rot and fear.

The first time I nearly lost my self again
as they felled ash and sycamore to let more light in
but less air.
You held my hand
when I couldn't remember if it was branch or limb,
held me down
screaming.

When I woke you taught me what your skin felt like
and how barkless flesh
could yield
as we fucked
in the most natural way
while a fox looked on,
bemused,
and though I'd taught you to be invisible
to all but the animals,
as I penetrated you
I'm sure the green-fingered nearly-witches
in the allotments
whose plants grow quicker than all the others
must have heard our moans.

As I listened to that heart of city and life,
stretched myself across the days,
you showed me there was time for love
even in spring
when there is no time for anything,
and how in winter
instead of growing stiff and moving only on the days
where light bursts in warm confusion through the city mists
I could be heated,
stay sap-fresh and flowing,
with fallen wood,
cotton and layered moss.

I remember when you moved in
to my triangle between buildings
and we grew together,
rooted ourselves,
wove spells into walls,
taught streams the secret paths
that the worms shared,
sang branch to life
and taught the trapped breeze
the words its mother told us.

It's today, my love,
a hundred years
after I took your hand.

Let's feed the rivers gold again
but let them wake this time
to writhe free from their prison.
Let's sing the bricks to clay,
teach the gulls our war cry,
guide roots to release their coiled wrath.
Let's tell the rats the colour of the sky
and help the city to remember
the endless forest.

GROWTH

when she returned from holiday
the professor found the students

had tricked her or maybe
listened to her better than she thought
but found the tree an elder

or at least that's what it looked like in the end
with its broken/ /set branches
skittering like an elder

but she had found that tree
that might now be an elder
turned upon its base
branches suffocating/ /luxuriating
in the damp soil
and
roots screaming fractals at the sun
or
maybe
breathing for the first time

the roots

or branches
now tried the air out
like a new way of walking

and unfurled small vicious leaves
into the sky

and the once
branches//roots
had presumably at least learnt to drink

whether
that professor was surprised
I cannot say

and as for the tree

well

nothing had changed

STEAK

pulling back the shower curtain
I find Jesus licking his lips with calf-
sized tongue and staring at the moistness
of my thigh I ask him to pass
my towel because that seems to be the
only thing to say and he does
but it is wrapped around a heart-shaped lump
of flesh

bite it

he says and I do flesh becoming
meat becoming blood-filled sponge and running
down my neck my nipples over pubes
off the reverence of my penis and
onto floor stepping forward he
holds my shoulders and then I think he kisses
me though I couldn't tell you where
or how long only that my chest leaks into
my arms in the way that it always
does when I receive a kiss
with all my being I open eyes that are
still light with water and check behind the
shower curtain the towel the drawers
for keeping the small bottles of shampoo
but there is no one and nothing but
pinkish water on the tile

HERO

ROUGE / ROGUE

for Susan Pevensie

She's interested in nothing now-a-days except nylons and lipstick and invitations.

She'd had the page passed to her by another soul
as she wandered the Asphodel Meadows.

She hadn't seen the final book before.
It made sense, though.
She'd felt his discomfort
as she was written into that second tale
at the thought that she was now old enough
to be bleeding freely onto his pages.

The boys had been having erections and wet dreams for years,
but it was that quiet trickle that had done it.
That and the makeup, which she had taken to wearing
for the joy of it,
or maybe it was just colour itself
in that world that was painted more leaf-mould brown
than people liked to remember
because of the talking animals.

Red was hers now entirely,
lips and fingers dipped into,
arrows feathered with it.

It was strange,
the single sheet ripped out alone,
and she signed it with a large lipstick kiss,
a scarlet O,
a rising sun.

MY FRUITIER THAN AVERAGE DAY

When I wake up
I am a banana.
Initially, when I wake up,
I am not actually aware that I am a banana,
think only of tea,
slide to the kettle,
stand swaying,
and because I am already long, and slightly bent,
it takes me a while to notice that today
I am, in fact, a banana.

I tell my boyfriend
that I am a banana today,
and though he can't see
what I would have thought was fairly obvious
he does believe me,
asks,
'Okay.
Have you ripened yet?'
I reply
that I have not
but later I might,
probably
will.

He says,
'Will work be okay,
in case you slip and fall
on some of that goopy stuff that leaks out
from the bottom of bananas
that are past their best-before date?'

'It'll be fine,'
I say.
'One: nothing's leaking out my bottom, thank you very much,
and
two: if my skin does split

they won't notice
and I can wear long socks
to keep the squidge
inside my shoes.
Better
than sitting here
waiting for the flies to land.'

Bananas ripen faster in bunches.
And the banana sitting next to me on the bus
is bruised,
her eyes darting faster and faster.
I wonder if they've started to spin
fully round
as she oozes ethylene
and I watch the skin on my arms
begin to lose its green.

Work is hard –
yesterday was fine,
but yesterday I was not a banana,
and as I have not been one for two whole weeks now
I was starting to hope
that I would never be a banana again.

Most of my friends who are fruit, you see,
are always fruit,
so sometimes I worry that I'm not allowed to call myself one,
which is stupid,
but as I said earlier – I am a banana
and my brains are literally mush.

Sometimes I wonder where my banana goes
when I am not being it,
and if, when I pull the tags of skin around my nails away,
they'll come off in long stripes,
yellow unfolding from beneath.

At one thirty-four
I go to lunch with my friend
who is an apple.
She is always an apple
and this is a very boring thing to be
because there are so many apples
everywhere
and these days, God, it just seems like *everyone's* an apple,
but nevertheless she is an apple
to the core.

People don't believe that she is an apple.
'I don't believe that you are an apple,'
they say.
'You are so firm and tart one minute
and then fall to mush in an instant;
how *can* you be an apple?'

'But that's what an apple is,'
she says,
'you are literally
describing an apple,'

and she is very patient,
she is very very patient.

She has long given up on not being an apple,
but she hopes today that by being in work,
outside,
away from home,
she can maybe at least
turn from mushed
to stewed apple,
which is a small
but significant improvement.

After work I go to the pub.
Drinking helps me feel less like a banana,
though the next day I often find

I have slipped on my discarded peel
and skidded so hard
straight into my old skin
that I am stuck being banana for at least two more days.

At the pub I meet a friend who used to be an orange
but is now a clementine.
We try not to talk about oranges
because every time
she hears oranges talk about being themselves
she can feel herself swelling back up with juice,
skin thickening
and pith between her lips again,
eroding the back of her teeth,
pulling at enamel
as the reek of citrus oil clings to the air.

My friend, who is a lime, joins us,
flopping into a chair.
He has squeezed himself
for other people
who do not want the whole of him
but find his zest endlessly fascinating,
pour it into their drinks at parties
and relish the taste,
leaving his shrivelled sour flesh
to dry out on the chopping board
in the corner of the kitchen.

Before we go
we are joined
by another friend
who is
a
tomato.

Obviously as
a
tomato

she knows how hard it is,
it is so *hard* being a fruit,
and so she tells us
all about it
despite the fact
she does not bruise
and is never put
in fruit salads.

She posts a lot on Instagram about being a fruit,
claims to be part of the fruit bowl.
She also claims to be a banana, and an orange,
depending on the audience.

I think she is a good person,
but I find it hard to be around her
as she tells me how intensely hard it is to be a banana
while I slip comically about the floor,
slowly turning bitter:
no, do go on,
please tell me what it's like.
The trouble is
she might not be a fruit
(though I wonder if maybe she is a secret apple),
but
even if she isn't
I accept that from a distance
it looks
juicy, maybe,
to be a fruit,
or at least
gives you identity, belonging
in some small way,
though I hope for her sake she can belong
without being a fruit
as I wouldn't wish fruithood
on anyone.

On the bus home I think about family.
My mum is an apple
and I was scared of being an apple
for a really long time.
She was convinced my brother and me
would also grow into apples,
but, as it turns out
sometimes the apple does fall far from the tree
and sometimes the apple
is a banana.

On the walk up my hill
I scratch myself on a hedge
and I realise that I am overripe.
It is only the tiniest scratch,
but all the yellow ooze
inside my head
flows out of me,
as inevitable and as forceful
as a tide of custard,
and I softly break in half,
and I am a banana,

and I am a banana
split.

My partner listens
as I vomit yellow at him
and explain
that I am dying,
I am dying now,
the hedge had a bird dropping on
which gave me flu
and tetanus
and maybe hepatitis,

and he calmly explains
that influ-tetan-titis
isn't a real thing

and I am not dying,
and I lug my chopped-up
flesh into bed
for the three hours left before midnight.

I don't sleep for another two hours,
but eventually I do,
and honestly, it's fine,
it's fine these days, but
I still hope that when I wake up
I am no longer a banana.

ABRACADABRA – THREE SPELLS FOR BANISHMENT

I

'Why does he look like that?' I asked, referring
to the man on the TV who was sat
splendid, riding on a white horse and
dressed in a coat that seemed to sing
with colour. What confused me
at age eight was the winged
makeup. My neighbour
saw me staring:
'He's gay,' that
splendid
thing.

II

It wasn't because they were gay, and only
said the once, but the gays they did know were
selfish. When my parents discussed them
on that long drive, they probably
didn't think twice about it
or know how easily
a child holds on to
thoughts carefully
and new words
selfish
ly.

III

The moment that I tell them, waiting to see
what they will say, then watching concern fold
over their faces, fear I will find
AIDS or violence, telling me
things I am already scared
of. I wish to be free
of these memories,
let them slowly
lose their hold
over
me.

SPLIT

I am
clawing at myself in the shower
till I am the colour of desecration and
puffy
till I feel like I could squeak like wet hair like childhood baths
staining
slickness
seeping out of me
congeals under my toes

knees conduct convulsions to the lino
as I curl and vomit
rhythmically
praying
in between each spasm

the nurse talks to me
and I use that old body ice
trick my father taught me without realising
to carry on
mouth caked with iron

for months my lack of forgiveness
is unforgivable to you
as I fail to follow your allowed schedule for anger
as time becomes obligation
not healer

when you later blame me
I know then
that swollen feeling
of squeaky cleanness
was the deepest cut I ever made
and that us taking six more months to die
should have surprised me more

BUBBLES

In the health food shop a boy with the most freckles
I have ever seen
asks,
'Are you brothers?'
and
*pop*
and it's really not his fault.

Later,
walking down Gloucester Road,
a woman smiles at us,
then smiles wider,
hugely,
and
*pop*
and I know it's Validation,
Praise,
Acceptance,
we are rare
like four-leaf clovers
or shiny Charizards
and hey, I'd smile too if I saw the same,
but right now
it is just another reminder.

Next time
a man stares
and stares
and stops walking
and scowls.
This time
it's cos of one little prick;
inevitably,
*pop*
it bursts.

*

You know *that* poem
you wrote in your head
or heard a thousand e-n-d-l-e-s-s times at open mic nights
about that hackneyed universal moment when,
'like,
you're dancing,
the bass is *so dense* it becomes your heartbeat,
bodies merge into the room
and you totally just forget yourself'?

But
they're kind of right,
aren't they?
That feeling.

For me
it's just
me
and you
wearing our yoga shorts
and stretching,
smiling,
togethermoves,
downward-facing dog,
salutation to the sun.
We laugh.
It is hilarious
and of course
intensely erotic
and we are perfectly us.

*

I think about these moments,
how the best we are at being ourselves
is in solitude,
when we walk on empty country paths,

not weighed down by other people's bitterness
or blown up and inflated
with any Expectations,
existing
just like every other couple.
Almost.

Really, though,
we're shutting out the world,
blowing a bubble around,
letting our otherness spread out and away.
Sure, the pearlescent soapy surface is beautiful,
but rainbows close up
all the time
are A Lot.
And I just want to breathe big
till the bubble grows wide
to green hills and horizons
and I can hold your hand
without being anything
at all
for a few hours more.

TRICKSTER

TOUCH ME – YOU WON'T BELIEVE WHAT HAPPENS NEXT…!

Hi!
How are you guys?
You all look very handsome
and it's so lovely to finally meet you.
Just one small request:
could you
please
touch me?

Go on.
Please?
Click me.
It won't take long.
No? Okay.
Fine.

Let me let you in on a little secret.
I know I said you're handsome,
but I could make you so much more.
Those teeth,
yellow and… furry,
I could whiten
in Five Easy Steps!

Click me.
I know I've just popped up, out of nowhere,
but it's just to let you know that you're the
Ten Millionth Virus.
I mean Winner!!
I mean You're A Winner!
You have Won.
Because you are the ten millionth visitor.
Not virus.
NO ONE'S A VIRUS.
And you can claim your prize
of Ten Laptop Apple

if you'd *just* click here.

Click me.
I'll smooth out your teeth.
SKIN!
And I'll whiten your cat.
I mean TEETH!
Unless you want that?
Do you want your cats whitening?
I can do that!
(You sicko.)
In seventy-eight **easy steps**.
Although…
is it…
lengthening
you want?
I can
L e n g t h e n.
Grow you Ten. Whole. Inches.
Make your cat *ten inches longer.*
Get your cat ripped.
I mean get you ripped with this one simple trick to get a six pack
get a 12 pack get a 25 PACK in Three. Easy. Weeks.

Click me.
I think there's been a misunderstanding…
If you just bring that cursor over here,
you'll see *I'm not an ad,*
I'm a
horny divorcee
in **your** area.
Now my husband's gone
I don't want love, I just want
GRANDMAS!
I mean,
I'm a horny CAT!
In **your Area**,
No, I mean
CLiCK mE

I just WANT
To show you **this video**:
Of Richard Dawkins, And This Puppy Who Are Best of Friends,
At 10 Seconds You'll Cry, At 30 you'll laugh, at 40 you'll
JOIN THE NAVY
click me

I'm sorry!
I'm new at this.
Please just let me show you
Ten Celebrities
Who Are Hiding Their Conjoined Twins with Contouring
OR tell you the ten easy tips for wrinkle-free teeth
I mean SKIN
told to me by this one RIPPED grandma,
WHO doctors HATE!!!

Just roll me back
and I'll set you up with
these Horny Cat Videos
in **your area**,
who all grew ten-inch puppies
with this one simple trick for MASSIVE TEETH!
dentists hate me.
moms **hate me**.
Richard Dawkins **h a t e s me.**
even HORNY grandmas in your area looking for love HATE ME
in three. easy. steps.

please?
click me
I just want
Love
Love
in
One
Easy
Step.

click me?

SLIPPERS

for Grandpa
after William Dickey

I found him in the garden
with a sun-bleached plastic deckchair
tying knots.

You know, he said, putting on clothes
and removing his nudity,
apart from these I don't have

much left. His fingers worked themselves
gradually faster. Each blue plastic string stood straight up
and scared.

Eventually, he finished, left his sea urchin kiss
scratched into my cheek and tied
the last balloon to the deckchair.

He rose quickly for such a warm day and was soon
passing behind a cloud
shaped exactly like Carol Vorderman's face.

BUS STOP

The man on the street is picking his nose,
not lost in thought
but married to the action,
catching his nails on the spurs inside
and alternating fingers on the right and left hand
for optimal picking.

The man on street
now flicks and brushes
hands down jeans,
front
                back,
crosses himself,
arms flowing to armpit,
heaves chest into bosom
and back,
sniffs   hands,

conscious.

Pauses,

like he has picked up my eyes,

but then sniffs armpit,
breathes back of hand,
re-drinks breath.

the man street
street man
now raise
arms
fake stretch sniff
bigger than sniff
man Snort
stuff hand to nostrils

armpit
          nostril
streetman folds hand
folds right hand down front
cups
slides left hand down line from back of back
to buttocks
between
burrows
now hands back face
now   fold   body
now pawing
                              roaring
snorts
             into hands
                              nostrils flap
nostrils fill
nostrils fill only
with man
with man man is only
man is onl
y

EVERYONE IS FASCINATED WITH MEN FUCKING MEN

i

the way our bodies come together
the rhythmic slap of thigh on buttock
is a sound effect that must by now have moved to the top drawer
of the BBC sound effects department

I wonder how they make *the sound of two men fucking*
and it is fucking
not making love
is it by punching an arm until it goes numb
by slapping two raw steaks into each other   with force

or is it with cabbages
I remember once someone telling me
that the sound effect for decapitation is
the captured moment of a cleaver
through a cabbage
is that how it is done
holding taut green meat in each hand and clapping
till you get that just right
sound of two men fucking

ii

stepping outside afterward
we all have an argument about it
friends reflect the question onto us
or ask around it until they think they have the answer
or wear it in their eyes
we know
they say
we've worked you out

we laugh, join in
cos my friend Anushka
she's a top for sure
and we both know
Kate's boyfriend couldn't be a hungrier
power bottom

and
I feel powerful and
guilty for a while

iii

I wonder how many of these directors have had period sex
or put a towel down

in *Brokeback Mountain* and *God's Own Country* they spit
once
and fuck
and the only way that would have worked is if Jake Gyllenhaal
and that vet
had the shits

but that's not what we want to watch, is it
sitting in an arts cinema
eating wasabi popcorn

OUT WITH IT

a man has pulled down his trousers
and begun to urinate on the floor in front of you and
while you would normally be okay with
a small amount of urination
described in a poem you
notice that the words on this page are now
gently speckled with piss in that light morning
dew on a tent way and that this mist is gradually
beading and
that the piss is sliding off the words and
onto your hands running down your wrists and
dripping onto the floor in fact this man is
thunderously peeing and this poem is now
saturated
pouring out with piss and the man is in the room
with you now
not just in the poem's room and the warmth
at the bottom of your toes is urine surging
up your trousers like an invading army and
when you try to run all you succeed in
doing is making the smell far stronger and
now the pee has reached your waist the pee
from this poem and
it is warm but not in an unpleasant way and
who'd have thought a man could urinate that much and
now the piss is above your shoulders and
this hot piss smoke is below your nostrils in your nostrils and
as you breathe in your lungs are filled with the stench
of piss but by now it has become strangely reassuring and
suddenly urine is over your head and
you are floating
hair like seaweed
and this poem has stopped

pissing all over everything

FAGGOT

GANYMEDE

he was
fresh honey in motion
an onion steeped in sunlight
or even just the shape of gold
or
simply
someone that you could meet for the first time
in a room bulging with people
but swear later that it had been just you
and him

we met
in a freshers' kitchen built out of damp and old milk
I can only remember his smile
and the moment that Sarah and I
both quietly fell in love with him

it was like floating
friendship with him
a warm bath a mile deep
bubbles like clouds
dawning bliss

in second year he told us
sheepishly
that he was dating
a thunderous man who had swooped him up
and it was hard not to be jealous
when our golden boy went away
for longer and longer weekends

we nagged to meet him
though there was never the time
but in the end we ran into them
and one of the boyfriend's many brothers
at the Red Lion

we hadn't realised how *old* they were till then
that brother with irises that screamed of drowning
but a smile like an apology
and Zeus himself
with a gaze like noon
blue
and touched with the threat of infinity

'he's different, you know?'
Ganymede told us
we knew
my palm ached from that handshake the week before
and our friend
had begun to wear clothes the colour of twilight
with long sleeves
despite the summer warmth

'he's married,'
he slurred later that night
'he's married and she hates me
and
I don't think I'm the first...'

but the next day
he was
fine
and forgetful

I rang a friend
whose sister had dated a god
and he told me
how she'd been
twisted
into a swan
and I thought of the midnight marks
on Ganymede's neck

I spoke to Sarah
and we decided to go camping for the weekend

just to get him away
and
it was like sunrise again
just us

until
Zeus walked
straight out of the night
whispered something in Ganymede's ear
and told us
that our friend was moving into Zeus's family home,
and Ganymede followed him into the evening air
with only one look back

much later
the brother knocked sheepishly on our door
and told us that Ganymede was hung across the heavens
as stars now

and even when I wear my glasses
I can barely see the golden shimmer
that he used to be

and I try not to think of a leering old man
pushing pins into corkboard
to hold up photos
of the men he used to fuck

CHEKHOV'S LOVER

> *'If you say in the first chapter that there is a rifle hanging on the wall, in the second or third chapter it absolutely must go off. If it's not going to be fired, it shouldn't be hanging there.'*
> Anton Chekhov

Act I

after we'd fucked
you placed him lightly on the mantelpiece
as you stood stark bollock naked
playing with something you'd picked up from the desk
I think that bracelet I got from Italy

'there's this new gay at work
you'd love him
he's kind of fit too'

there was something almost
forcedly casual
as you
stood there
buttocks gleaming
playing with my bracelet
and stroking the idea of him
with all the caution and care you would give
to a loaded gun

Act II

maybe it was already inevitable
the universe or whatever gods there are
had noticed it placed there on the mantelpiece
loaded
and your mind had mapped out
the office fantasies and swollen moments
made it real
your hands brushing over a hole punch

your twin streams of urine
gently caressing each other
in the shared urinal

Act III

there was a thrill in it too
as the tension mounted and I looked round to check that yes
it was still there
steel grey and sticky with cold
there's no real danger without a loaded gun
and now I'm wondering if I should use it first
running my fingers around the rim of the elegant cocktail
that has appeared in my hand solely for the purpose
of this extended metaphor
as I circle the room
bringing myself back towards the pistol
yearning to feel the reassuringly dangerous
weight of it in my hands

HO HO HO

'Twas the night before Christmas
And all through the house
Just one thing was stirring
And it wasn't a mouse.

See, that fine Yule night I was sipping mulled wine
And feeling so very alone,
And, just like a dog who needs something to gnaw on,
I too yearned for a bone.

It's then I see up on the mantelpiece
On the front of a Christmas card
Something red and round that gets me quite warm
And makes my toy soldier ha...ppy.

Oh, God, I must have been knocking it back,
Cos when I set eyes on Saint Nick...
I don't tend to go for elderly men,
But golly, I ache for his... pork pie.

But Santa's not real and I'm all alone,
Though are those hooves on the roof, I wonder?
And with no further ado he comes   down the flue
With a bang, and a laugh, and a thunder.

Now that he's here I'm certain and sure
That he is the one that I lust for.
His spherical shape makes my knees start to quake
And my trousers drop down to the floor.

With a twinkle in eye, he grabs a mince pie
And rubs crumbs all over his belly.
He rips off his top and reveals a lot
Of grey fur and a whole bowl of jelly.

My soldier stands to attention
And nods his small wooden head.

Saint Nick lifts me, so gentle and strong,
And brings me right up to bed.

He lays me down amongst the crisp sheets
And gives me a soft tender kiss,
And from that point on
My memory fades,
But I think it went something like this:

*

Grey hairs, sweaty gut,
Crumb-filled belly button fluff
And oh my God, oh, what a butt,
My sexy Daddy Christmas.

Hairy balls, hairy back,
Hairy fucking hairy crack,
Soon he'll have an empty sack,
My sexy Daddy Christmas.

His Yule log rears its mighty head.
It's not just Rudolph glowing red.
Shove my face into the bed,
My sexy Daddy Christmas.

Right there, oh yes! Oh gOsh That's Right!
There's no more chance of silent night,
But OH we might just make it white,
My sexy
Daddy
Christmas.

*

When I awake on Xmas morn
I clutch my aching head.
I can't remember much last night.
Is this a… carrot in my bed?

My package is quite tender,
I fear for my bum,
And in my mouth there is no doubt
That that's the taste of… Christmas spices.

I've had it up to here
With all this Christmas smut.
There's tinsel round my todger,
And a… bauble up my butt?

My whole body aches,
I reek of festive spice.
I can't quite decide,
Was I naughty… or nice?

TARMAC

it is fascinating watching men yield
like when tarmac melts
pungent too
sweat and bitumen hang heavy
it is fascinating

I see one man
while wives are at the bar
caress his friend's ear unconsciously
and the unthinking subject lean into large cupped hand
and breathe

it makes me wonder
if I have cast them wrong
but they wake
crack apart
look round
sweat
and resume
their spousal roles

for a moment there
I saw
a softness not often seen
muscles relaxing

I doubt they are like me
but fear of it
prevents those briefest of touches
the most important ones
when we stand together

completely naked

INNOCENT

PLEASE REMEMBER THAT THE STATIONERY IS FOR OFFICE USE ONLY

The man in the office is wearing a blue shirt.
He is wearing a blue shirt because he knows that eventually we will all die
and, that being the case,
he will never wear white shirts, because they remind him too much of boarding school.

The man in the office is wearing a blue shirt.
It is the exact colour that all blue shirts must be
if you are a middle manager, which he is,
but want to show that you are not uptight,
like all those white, and even cream, shirt wearers.

The man in the office is wearing a blue shirt.
He hopes that the blue will not show the shape of his nipples through the fabric,
like so many of his white shirts,
which now lie in the cleaning rag pile, because his cousin Jenny,
who is his cousin on his mother's side,
pointed out how large they are, for a man's nipples.

The man in the office is wearing a red shirt.
He is wearing it because it is dress-down Friday,
or perhaps he is feeling like a little change,

or because it is nearly Christmas and red is, after all, festive,
or maybe he thinks that his sweat patches are less obvious when they are red,
which they aren't,
though no one would think to say that to him.

The man in the office is wearing a grey shirt.
It is slightly too big, with short sleeves, in the exact grey of boarding school plimsolls,
with a single stripe on the left-hand side, to add a touch of fun.
It is a light grey that not only shows his armpit sweat clearly
but advertises the fact that backs can also sweat at least as much again.
It is the kind of shirt he would wear only if nothing else were clean,
or if he were suicidal,
and possibly out of clean clothes as well, as these things do tend to coincide.

The men in the office are wearing white shirts.
They can see each other's nipples, unless they've paid for the thicker cotton,
which serves to neatly sort the managers from the rest.
They mainly hate their white shirts,
except, of course, for the IT department
and the few that enjoyed boarding school,
but colour is too festive now,
and grey is not something they would wear again.

TRANSLUCENT

garlic skin slides off the plate
as the water
finishes turning brown
from a cake that took most of the afternoon to make

the water is Goldilocks warm
but greasy so the bubbles have almost gone
and brown   like cake

your hands are in there
stopped
the window is fogged
steam thick
the window needs cleaning
probably
and that is   a woman
in the street
with
a child

there is the sound of breathing
in the kitchen
and it is steady
loud
you think you can smell
smell
the cumin
from last night
small and sharp in your nostrils

sharp

it would be easier if she had said –

the woman in the street
the mother
has picked up something dropped

carelessly
by the child

the breathing is there still
the boiler clicks on
off
but the kitchen is full of silence
despite the noise

– if she had said *die*
maybe it would have been easier

and the water is cold now

her want to not exist
nothingness

how can you still smell cumin
through all this

to want because it's too much otherwise
those notes in the voice
of certainty
and

and you have cold brown greasy water on your T-shirt

and the child
and mother have gone
or moved behind
the fogged-up part

and you are not sure how long you have been standing here
crying

INHERITANCE

It is Thursday.
Payday.
We are in the only place to be on payday
and, of course, there are men,
although really
if you peer past that perfumed haze of voice, ale and spittle
and look
you'll see
these are boys,
boys drinking,
boys drinking till their fathers fall out of their mouths
and punch words across the bar:
'Did you see her
knock-me-down-and-rape-me heels?'
his father says,
veins popping in his nose
as knuckles grip teeth
and he rebirths himself from his own son's mouth.
Agreement comes harmonious
as other men emerge from throats
that are sticky and loose with the sweetness of malt.
Fathers
pushing boys backwards
into shadows and grime-soaked leatherette seats,
laughing at things they don't believe.

Eventually one boy stands
and walks…
                    staggers,
bringing his father with him, and, of course, his drink.
He sips almost gently, as he sways above the urinal
and holds the glass up high
so he can't see his mother staring out
from grime-smeared mirror.

It is still Thursday,
it is two hours later

and there are men,
men drinking, old men, young men,
drinking till their fathers fall out of their throats
and keel over,
too drunk to stand,
too drunk to punch,
too drunk to remember their lines,
and slowly
as the fathers fade away at their feet
there are men
free,
men speaking
loudly,
quietly,
to friends,
saying,
'The doctor said it might be serious,'
or,
'When I hold my baby it won't stop crying,'
or,
in a whisper,
'It still hurts where she hit me,'
and then there are men
weeping
silently
with hugs that are three seconds too tight
and chests that swell,
starved.

It is no longer Thursday
and men have woken,
downed water to ease their swollen throats
and ignored last night's acid in the pit of their chests.
These are men
who are tired,
who have dragged themselves to work,
stewed and sweated
and returned home.
It is Friday evening now

and there is a boy, who is a man, who is a father,
and he is drinking
slowly
cautiously
in front of the TV.
And as the ache fades from his throat
his son comes in with bruised knees from bike ride,
crying,
and without thought
that dad, that tired boy drinking
says,
'Man up, kid.
It'll be fine.
Just have a sip of this.'

PARDON

the door of the cubicle leaves a gap
where you can see loose sheets of toilet paper
water swelling over the floor, or perhaps piss
and though you could come back tomorrow
a hand is placed across your chest by your hunger
for the briefness of a faceless body

taking communion, filling your mouth with blood and body
on your knees, lips bridging the gap
between you and him, mouth watering as if in hunger
pubes tearing out as your control rips like paper
hairs that you will pick from your teeth tomorrow
remembering the taste, under his foreskin, of old piss

that day, you see one standing too long to piss
the opposite of release in the clasp of his body
looking for a memory to hold for tomorrow
if only you'd seen in his eyes that yawning gap
before he drew, from his pocket, ID papers
laughing as you froze, half-knelt in hunger

they make you wait till you are nothing but a line of hunger
till you are swollen with piss
make you sign your name on a piece of paper
take from you your body
you wake in a cell with a head full of gaps
and no more tomorrows

and no more tomorrows
until suddenly there is public hunger
for a sorry, but you can see the gap
that a thousand apologies won't fill, like pissing
in the ocean, reality is ungoldened and your body
remembers when cops beat you like they were making paper

Thatcher wanted to keep warnings out of newspapers
defend decency, take away tomorrow
for so many, there were so many bodies
that shrivelled in hunger –
she wanted to stick the posters where we piss
flyers marinating where the cubicle door leaves a gap

through the gap in my front door a paper
sorry came today. I will piss on it tomorrow
when I have fed my hunger with this once-indecent body

VILLAIN

UNFUCKABLE

'Femme,'
his fingers splayed with the counting
each bent further than he will allow wrists to,
or himself,
'and, like, nothing against them, but not too Asian.'

He licks his lips, which are chapped,
but not from kissing fat men or poor men
or too-Asian men,
and will remain chapped until balm comes in masc.

Boredom hangs on his face, but gently,
for me to see,
underlined with cinema smile.
He has put Thoughts into this.

'Your face is fatter now,'
though he only notices it cos he's lost weight,
look how much weight he's lost,
it's from the gym, which isn't expensive
and is a good way to meet friends like him.

Four fingers. Four long fingers stopped
at the fourth thing he'd never fuck,
he frowns at his thumb –
'There's a fifth one, I know there is.
It's not black guys, though.
Great sex, but of course
I'd never date one.'

THIS CHARMING MAN

He was a boy,
she was
a
six-by-three-by-three block of marble;
can I make it any more obvious?

He was lip-bitingly – no,
lip-crushingly
sexy
with eyes of smooth brown soulful tenderness
and a beard you could… drown in?

He was a stone mason.
Like all high craftsmen these days,
he was on Instagram.
You know the stuff:
Just a little vid of me getting my rock on
#instagranite #rockoutwithyourchiselout

He was
not particularly fond of women,
not in *that* way
but more
just fed up
of all the girls
who just don't get him,
you know?
#lonelylifebeinganartist
#thestonecallsmewhydoesntshe

But one day
this hotel
commissioned him for his biggest project yet:
a beautiful
sexy
stoney lady.

He gets to work carving,
puts up these really long
timelapses on Instagram
while listening to some really obscure music
by this indie band you've probably never heard of
called The Smiths

and
I mean
he may use too many hashtags
and have myriad unresolved issues with women
but he is extremely good at sculpture
and before he knows it
he has carved
the most beautiful woman
he has ever seen.
#myperfectwoman #shesgotastoneyheartbutsodoalltheothers

And he's supposed to give her to the hotel
but he can't bring himself to.
He doesn't even
post about her on Instagram.

Well,
not as much as normal, anyway,
cos she feels
special.

And he pines,
and I mean really pines –
you know, the whole
black screen social media
woe-is-me kind of thing
ambiguous statuses on Facebook,
Why is love so hard? –
and he listens to this really obscure song
that you wouldn't know called
'Girlfriend in a Coma.'

Until one day
a goddess – Aphrodite –
was scrolling through Instagram
until she saw his posts
and followed him
and was like,
Damn,
he's hot
and so's that statue,
and, as goddesses do,
decided to give it life.

Imagine it for a second:
she stood
as statues do,
modestly,
when suddenly
stone warmed,
mouth trembled
and, from her lips,
'Fuck, it's cold!'

He was delighted,
you can imagine:
#dreamsdocometrue
#thatfeelingyougetwhenyoucreateyouridealwomanfromstone andshecomestolife
#relatable

It went well at first.
It was as if they were made for each other,
which was half-right anyway,
and their relationship
was
#couplegoals
#thatchiselthough
#shesbloodymarblelous

and it was supposed to be

happily ever after,
but,
well.

It started with her making friends,
which was fine with him, of course,
fine with him,
fine   with   him,
but don't be back late.

Of course
I love you.

Um, but
don't wear that.

You don't need makeup.
I made you perfect,
babe,

and I wouldn't eat that;
you already weigh the exact right number of stones,

and then
eventually

he even grew jealous of the sun
for daring
to give her wrinkles,

and, well, to cut a long story short,
he started listening to this really obscure artist
called Morrissey

and posting
pictures of sunsets
#somiserable
#womenareallthesameevenonesmadefromstone
#recentbreakup

or just a photo of an empty park swing
#imadeherheartandthenshetookmine
#selfishex

and she,
she
went off and lived life
and aged as messily and as happily as she could,
ended up writing for The Guardian
about the male gaze
and commodification of women,

finding readers who, despite her marble origins,
found something infinitely relatable about her.
You know,
How my ex made me from stone
and trapped me in a repressive relationship
and how in the end I escaped and got boulder
that kind of thing,
with absolutely no hashtags
or obscure musical accompaniment
of any sort.

IT NEVER RAINS BUT IT POURS

written based on the above prompt – with thanks to Chris

There was a minute there,
when I pushed the twin blades of the scissors
through the 267th kitten's leg
and it looked up at me with its wee little kitty eyes and mewed sadly,
that I thought,
Is this a little cruel?

There was a second there
as I cut through yet another cat's ankle
and collected the end bit into a bucket,
that I thought,
Is this entirely necessary?

There was an instant there,
when I loaded the dismembered cat hands into the catapult
and fired them into the clouds just as it began to drizzle,
that I wondered, *What am I doing?*

but then I take my job
as an actualiser
of homophonic idioms
incredibly seriously,

and you know what it *sounds like* they say,
I thought
as the bloody cats' feet fell from the clouds
and splattered onto the ground around me:

it never rains
but it

paws.

DEVIL'S DYE

From 1577 the German government prohibited the use of Asian indigo as it was bluer than the native woad-based blue dye. In 1609 Henry IV of France also forbade indigo under pain of death.

'It's bluer than ours,' the courtier said,
running the fabric through his fingers, blue
like the idea of water, blue,
like memories of rivers, blue,
like a child's painting, blue.
The problem was, of course, that what he said was true;
everyone in the court could see it.
They clustered in that way that peering people do,
held back by railings
bulging, like a man's thick stomach at his waistband.

It was bluer than ours, that blue that wasn't ours,
that wasn't ours, yet that we could buy, could own,
but couldn't make, our soil wrong.
Its blueness scorned our land.

The priest in the court crawled forward.
'It's bluer than ours,' he said,
'this devil's dye.'
The king, who was not a clever man,
dabbed honeylike sweat from his brow
and banned that hallowed blue.

It was too late though, as these things often are
and indigo caught fast in the minds of the court,
It's bluer,
in the heart of the trader that brought it there,
It's bluer,
where traces still lingered in the creases of her hands,
from that first washing,
that dyeing-birthing of it,
than ours.

And in a way that priest was right:
the hunger was devilish,
spread gleefully
from person to person,
fast as a secret in its telling
and loud like a secret too,
dancing, yelling from the corner
with no regard for manners.

It's bluer than ours,
went the tale,
and the memory made *our* blue dull,
as that other blue refused to fade,
growing in minds
till even the idea of it, the whisper
made our blue pale,
like wilting flower, blue,
like drowning ocean, blue,
like corpse cheek, blue.

The king,
mindful of the loudness of the spaces between words,
of the growing hunger,
like of springtime seeds for rain,
that king
banned our blue, too,
snatched shawls from widows,
blankets from babes,
collected it in mud-dark oak barrels
and locked it in the cellars of the castle.

It didn't work
and when flowers grew in spring
we remembered blue that wasn't ours
and screamed at the castle gates for it,

till flowers
were ordered
dug up,
                    poisoned,
                                        burnt,

but even babies' eyes were taste enough,
so the irises of children were tattooed green
by order
or torn out by mobs seeking that bluer thing that wasn't ours,

until suddenly
there was only the sky,
desperately close
and arrogantly blue,
and the sea and the rivers that flowed into it,
tempting now
and blue enough that some would never leave it,
and hundreds drowned from hunger
as they swam in blue
it was bluer than this
till they couldn't swim anymore.

And so the king
had two great taps made
of strong black iron,
placed one at the tip of the highest mountain
where the bottom of the sky whispered to the snow
and one fixed at the shore
where blue-starved bodies floated,
and the king's men turned the taps
and drained the turquoise from the sky,
the navy from the sea and from the rivers
that flowed between them,
and the octopuses, who, as you know, see only in blue,
floated in shock
as blue poured from the taps for days,
was rammed into strong oak barrels
and buried in the deepest cellar of the castle
where it was too deep to even see,
to even be,
bluer than anything.
We forgot then,
with the blue gone,
what blue was,

except when we dreamed
in colour,
which is the way we all dream, really,
but forgot on waking,
and sometimes would find ourselves crying
deep, belly-deep sobs
and none of us could understand
why thousands of tiny octopuses
had crawled out of the ocean
and died.

It was years later
that a spider,
who had crept into the deepest cellar of that castle
to write the novel she had promised to write years ago,
but because of her thousands of children
just hadn't had the time,
tripped against a dark oak barrel,
which
cr/a/ /c/ked.

No one remembers what happened next,
but days later,
when the dust had settled,
we stood sheepishly in a ring around the sprawled guts
of that foolish king,
promised to never speak again of certain things,
and the ban on indigo was quietly lifted
as the world sang blue again

and the spider who had broken the barrel
couldn't see what all the fuss was about,
as, like all spiders,
she had only ever seen
in green and violet.

AN AFTERTHOUGHT

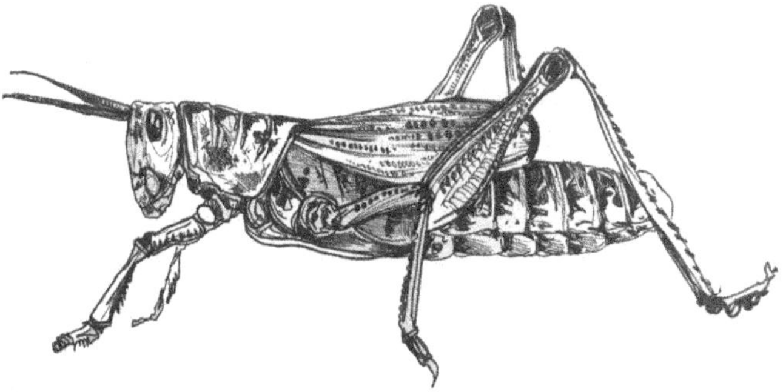

'I must write,' said the woman to the grasshopper. 'For I feel my skin drawing inwards with the years, falling round about me like the disguise of an old person.'

The grasshopper bowed a single feeler. It seemed sympathetic, without the normal hint of disdain that people hold for the old.

The woman was unsure whether the grasshopper was really understanding. She couldn't gauge its age by looking at its size or colour, and so far it wasn't telling.

'And,' she continued, 'if I write, I might yet find that secret part of me which is entirely unique.'

She paused, and the grasshopper looked up expectantly.

'That is to say, if I am unique?'

This was the bit that troubled her most. It was especially hard to say out loud, she decided, as she thought about that precious centre, her crystal heart through which she saw the world.

'We all have them,' she said at last. 'But I know, and not in the sense of arrogance, but I know that mine must be somewhat special.'

After all, she reasoned, if she knew about them, she was already miles ahead.

'The lens that sees lenses,' said the woman to the grasshopper.

The grasshopper inhaled, the better to soak up her wisdom.

'I see your lens, you see,' she said.

The grasshopper agreed. She really did have a sage-like grasp of his inner nature. It was reflected in her eyes.

'But,' the woman said, 'how to explain myself, my wisdom shared?'

It would be hard conveying it, and even if she were successful, she felt like it was the type of knowledge that, once you knew it, you thought you had always known.

'If anything, people will only hate me for it,' she said.

The grasshopper nodded; he already resented that she had thought of it first. He would have stolen the idea if it wasn't for the fact that by the time he had written it down and found a publisher he would probably have died of old age.

He conveyed as much to her by moving his back legs together very fast.

The woman frowned irritably. The grasshopper was very out of tune.

'Maybe writing is not for me,' she said, as if she hadn't heard the grasshopper. 'Maybe I will be ephemeral!'

She liked that thought. She could be a perfectly wonderful person, who played melodious music, smiled like she knew a great secret, and then was gone, but remembered forever.

She would use her insight to help others grow, and be the dedication in hundreds of books. *'...who taught me to be my truest self,'* or similar, was how they would read. It would be an untroublesome life. She smiled.

It must be easy being a grasshopper, the woman thought, but didn't say aloud to avoid offence.

And together they sat in silence for the rest of the afternoon.

ACKNOWLEDGEMENTS

It is always impossible to know all of the people you should thank, a list that you come back to again and again, desperate to make sure everyone who was a part of this is included.

Thank you to the many people who have read my work and given their sage advice: Malaika, Melanie, Thommie, Jo, Siân, Tom, Stef, Josie, Danny and Claire, to name a few.

Though I ended up doing biology, particular thanks should be given to my English teacher, Marty Bromfield, who helped me learn to *think* about writing, so that years later I had the tools to actually write.

Thank you to Dad for the support and calmness, and thanks to Mum for all those writing genes and the advice and wisdom to use them well.

Thank you to all at Burning Eye for believing in my work and for their support, and for all the poets who recommended me to them. Thank you especially to my editor, Harriet. Thanks as well to Jasmine Thompson, who did all of the beautiful illustrations. Thank you to the Milk team, to Beth, Sam and Malaika. Thank you to friends who have supported me in so many ways.

Thank you to Bristol. My writing has emerged during my time living here, and the many talented poets who live in and around the city are an inspiration. I haven't written much about Bristol herself, but if you need a cityscape to think of when you read 'Green' please think of Bristol, a place always on the verge of exploding back into a magical wilderness, and very much where the poem is set.

This collection is dedicated to Joy Denbigh, my grandma, who died during the course of me writing it. She was one of the first people to introduce me to myths, legends and fairytales, and kept sending me books my entire life. Joy was an extraordinarily wise and caring woman who loved and accepted me unconditionally. May there be more like her. Thank you.

Finally, I'd like to thank Jon, of course, for everything.

Lightning Source UK Ltd.
Milton Keynes UK
UKHW011421131119
353457UK00002B/246/P

9 781911 570721